I0539175

ISBN 979-8-218-75168-5

A Soul's Tree Speaks

Cover photo by Sean Money &
Elizabeth Faye Photography

Opening Haiku by Natasha Akery

Poetry allows me to carry the weight of the world forward rather than taking it home.

When there's an onslaught of exit signs, you learn to create a welcoming space.

A transformation tool for pain and anger to become art – a gift to humanity and my country.

fury folds
beneath the feet
of love

Death

(Commissioned by WE Coast Studios,
performed on November 9, 2024, for
Ritual & Release)

I love that there's butterflies in
September
Bumblebees still in the hunt for
pollen like spring
to appreciate them
we must tolerate the
mosquitoes who thrive off the
same ecosystem
yet somehow stay around long
after their expiration

What's more delusional?
Fearing death or aiming to live
to a hundred?
If we knew everything about
everything we wouldn't believe
in magic

Death is nothing short of an old
friend checking in
what we lose we regain
Perhaps the purpose of pets
is to remind us to live again
for we will surely outlive them

The unknown. The pain.
That's what we really fear
not the freedom of belonging to
a full circle
our energy renewed into the
stars we're enamored to view
Our skin. Our bones.
Naked napping back into
nature's lap

The passing of someone we
love is a passage —
a voyage we don't want them
to take alone
so, we store their bodies in
boxes or hold onto their ashes
somehow tragic or too soon

We fear letting go
not the freedom of belonging to
a full circle
What's more delusional?
Fearing death or aiming to live
to a hundred?

To embrace as an old friend
checking in is to live a life of
fulfillment
what you take you return
relearned from our births

Wishing upon stars
in awe of their decomposition
as they paint the sky
And oh,
how we wish on their deaths
so we can stay afraid to be alive

How silly that sounds
how silly that sounds
to make a wish without death
silly as Butterflies in September

The Marigolds Keep Lying to Me
(featuring Natasha Akery)

the marigolds keep lying

to me — there's no hope

seeking balance

in empty pockets

red clay on white soles

the canyon was a clean slate

wind encourages flowers to
laugh

I thought they were dancing

you can't take the rocks

the marigolds keep lying

to me — empty promises

only easy perception

strong enough to be a woman

flowers made you stay

sing a little song

maybe you'll forget the way

in deep conversations

1998 (featuring Mary Ross)

hope, promise, dreams, goals
back in 1998
we were happy then

twelve years old, relearn the
world music, dance, languages,
yoga, nap

the trail twists and turns
the marsh keeps calling me
salty water song

embrace universe
countries are calling me, why
hide in holy city hymns

if I plant that lemon tree
then I'm never gonna leave

triumph trauma garden
say hello to twelve years old

worldly spirit home

Seeing Us for the First Time

"I don't really know you."
So we went out for light fare,
errands and a walk
juggling our awkward
personalities quirks
separated entities once of
familiarity

I see so many her age
as she once saw me
get wrapped up in virtual
games and tv
overwhelmed by new lingo
table-turning thoughts
as I'm afraid to let her go

I worry about her as she once
worried about me

watching me warp from
technology
flowing with language
an adult across the table
she lets go of me

We smile
seeing us for the first time

As she got in the driver's seat
and placed her hand on the
door,
*"I'm proud of you. You worked
hard and I mean it."*

We go opposite directions
until we cross the corner of
a mother and daughter finding
each other

Farmer's Front Porch

Face paint and fruit
Sweet scents of lavender
basil honey
Nature's own candle
Musicians come and go
Sometimes the only social
interaction is a Sunday…

…sitting on Adam & Meghan's
front porch.

Fiber (featuring Mary Ross)

Those cotton shirts
Bear witness
To the fiber of his being

Watered weighted windows to
the soul
Missing your fibers on my
fingers
Another story on the shelf

Watered weighted windows to
the soul
Bear witness
To the fiber of his being
Those cotton shirts
Another story told

The only difference between a weed and a flower is judgement —
unknown

Tumble Weed

You picked weeds
You picked me
You never more

Discarded on a walk
Discarded for a rose
Discard now my ego

Left to wilt
Left to weep
Left to myself

After bursting through concrete
just to be seen
After blossoming through
growing pains you didn't see
After judgement decree, I still
care for me

Delicate yet everlasting
Delicate yet resilient
Delicate yet determined

Starts with one color
Starts with hazel eyes
Starts a new chapter

Oxidizes another
Oxidizes love
Oxidizes hurt

Thank you for picking this
weed
You helped set free

Home

is holding you in
a hammock under stars

Home is
holding your hand

Home is
a no-phone zone
where the only
vibrations are our hums

Home is
the silence in our
presence
that becomes the perfect
push to pursue projects

Home is
showing love
even when fear creeps
up from before

Home is
        forever
        but with you it feels like
        final hours

Visa-Free

a difficult composition
at a time when we finally
managed peace
placed in a position
where our friendship is
questioned — a liability

I don't pry into your personal
affairs outside of what you
share
often misunderstood
by whispers of your former self

this turbulence
has left me with an inability to
trust
seeking the definition outside
of a financial institution

take accountability for
carelessness
especially when your highs
make it easy to forget

Watching this friend-ship sail
once an anchor — gusty
grievances, harbored hearts,
family feasts
letting you go
is the hardest to cast

how did we get to this foreign
land once familiar?
welcome broke down to
'well, how come you're here?'

honesty
transformed as transportation
security:

Passport?
Reason for your visit?
Length of stay?
Emotional baggage?

while you walk in visa-free
I bear the cost of this interaction

6/24/2024 11.45 pm

The piece you seek is really the truth
The piece you seek is the peace
Your missing piece is your inner piece.
Your missing piece is your inner peace.
Your missing piece is your inner peace.

We are addicted to being the way
we are —Don Miguel Ruiz

Rhythm of Rest

At morning's first light
we reach for a visual aid
instead of allowing
our vision to aid us
recharge our phones well
before our own bodies

Caffeinated chokeholds
seeking inspiration in
publications
flashing
oppressed opinions
seizures of scripts
that attempt
to shred the tapestries of our
narratives

We believe no one
understands us
we all sing the same song
terrified to let people know

how broken we are on the
inside
we state we're fine
closed hearts eyes blind

Our negative thoughts have
something in common:
they make us the problem
falsifying medication as
meditation

We tell ourselves,
get dressed
unaware
that we're too depressed
to address
our calls for distress
individuality disguised as
illness

Memories missed
by our overworked shifts
a high tolerance for pain isn't
an invitation to bear it

we freed ourselves from
kingdoms
but buried our history between
the lines of democracy and
dictatorship

Discard the materials that make
up your sword
forgo the emotional compass
you call happiness
for the missing piece you seek
is your inner peace

Eager to accept our illusions vs
embracing our light
how did our best gift become
our greatest fear
like a fly caught in confusion
choosing to stay in prison
when the door is wide open

Shattered Glass

break ups are heartbreaking
or liberating either way
leading you back to
soul searching

unintentional hurt
while healing
racked up reams of paper
crushed by the weight
scabs of paper cuts
still bleeding

glass full or empty
either way cracking
do you glue it together
or simply replace it

what once held us
now in fragments

temporarily broken down
for you to see
there's light in everything

life isn't falling apart
if you still have a beating heart
we're fixated on what once was
deflecting the possibility
of something else
once seemed impossible

Imprint

I hear them say,
"Not my tree, not my problem"
"My yard, my space"
decades later descendants fight
over the same fence
desiring to taste the bearing
fruit

I keep silent like woodpecker
who keeps brisk flight
never sings in its presence
gaining confidence in
this tiny feather against a giant
tree

My early morning pecks are
those that I type
we chip away
Bird in bark

and, I, in book
doting daily against despair

Those who plant trees are
loving
Those who built fences hold
fear
The fruit it bares is
beautiful
holding negative words
an invisible poison
false seeds absorbed by the tree

I don't recall ego in ecosystem
of all the birds that sing their
arrival not woodpecker or even
hummingbird
Their rhythm echoes in the
heavenly scent of morning
the break between reality and
divinity

not to tear the tree down but
remove its negativity
sip on sweet nectar

my rest is a testament to my
protest
I will not burn buildings of
which others made
or books bound to be read
Nor will I film
Nor will I fear
Nor will I fuel
the fire that comes for us all but
meant for the tree

Woodpecker and I will leave
imprints
In the roots
In the rings
In the dust

a reminder of feathers
what we can do together

My Two Sense

We are not mind readers
therefore we made blinkers
Yet used *after* slowing down
and merging

We get text messages from
spam and shipping
Not
opting for signals of road
closures and legal policies

If it's not a contest
we care less
A representation of our nation
doing things that don't make
sense

Heal from Hate

I know people on both sides
a weaver of documented stories
placed in their eyes
I can see why
immigrants vote the other guy
risking deportation

I can feel how
little girls place hope in one
they carry this weight
forgetting they can be anything

Our obligation is to be better
than our elected
Our differences create possible
impossibilities

Where we failed
collectively is diplomacy

continuing to argue, accuse, assume
Emotionally Driven Train Wrecks
as the world watches our tantrum

The unnecessities of
banning books vs reading them

When did boys wearing tutus become taboo or girls getting gritty in the dirt?
allow them the freedom to be free before we force them to be adults

Children confusing the written alphabet
as their chosen gender
well before developed bodies
more concerned over pronouns

then the compassion of
a human being...
...learning English for the first
time

Consumed   by   product
propaganda
from what we eat
to how we medicate
we forgot how to heal
ourselves from hate

Change begins within self
Change   reflects   our
communities
well before it reaches a nation

If we continue,
if we allow our emotions to run
away,
will good mornings evaporate?

Too many preachers out of
practice of purpose
piece together peace
before it cracks you

While so many choose to wake
up angry and afraid
I choose to wake up
say good morning
and heal from our hate

Shaped Reflections

we carve mirrors to match
everybody's curve
hours melting glass
designing the frame to hold the
most divine work of art
— You

the weight of seeing one's
reflection turns our work into
fragments
can you recognize self-love?

the truth hidden
under layers of skin products
the copious comments

full circle the frame
right color for the room
wrong for your weight

the weight
of seeing your reflection
turns our work into fragments
can you recognize self love?

artists
pick up your pieces
broken glass
ripped pages

transforming
your depression
into expression

Mosaic II

(Commissioned for HALO's *Singers & Stanzas*, a collaboration of poetry and music, debuted on May 4, 2024 — written and spoken by Duran, sung by Lindsay Metzger, and composed by Laura Jobin-Acosta)

Forgotten

Colors painted under your dust
covered veil

Their feet trapped you in time

Forgive them

Most importantly

Forgive yourself

Under Islamic mosaics

A crafter knowingly creates
hidden mistakes

No greater is he over the Divine

You are the indent within the
imagery

The purposeful prose upon
which we sing

Ingrained in my memory

A worldly incompletion

For their un-dedication

Lacking the love, you chose to
give

Forgive them

Most importantly

Forgive yourself

A part of me died with you

Your absence, an impact

Perhaps it is me who needs
forgiveness

Failing to see the cuts of your
chards

Under masked glass

Your pattern infinitely etched
in my mind

Beautifully placed with design

You are the indent within the
imagery

The purposeful prose upon
reminding us

We are humanity.

Barakah

the past is a museum
a collection of gifts unopened
forgetting to unlock our minds
the key to our potential
the godliness in all of us
dispersed through specks of
time weighed by the memories
we keep

forgotten feelings of falling
asleep
eyes closed in clarity
creating a cadence of calm
like leaves in a lazy river
no alarm to beware
just ahh ware

the difference between
always and forever is the
spelling
neither is definite
in an infinite universe we
barely grasp

/ / /

does discovering your purpose
make for shorter days?
a ticking time bomb
or
a lottery for some
why do so many in opportunity
choose to stay mentally
oppressed while the
physically oppressed
have no term for expression?

the sirens transcend
bombarded by the media
anxiety is now the new rhythm
in a space where memories
once lived
torn down
where did they go?

/ / /

Listen
listen to the stories expressed in
explosives
stories so loud
even America's birthday can't
drown them out
breathe them in,
so thick hanging in nuclear
perfume

the weight of creating
happiness
does the opposite
boundary restrictions
physical placements
mental statements
divided diversity
were we not born of God's
creation?

///

losing sight in our futures
we've omitted our
presence
forgotten our past
counting what we have
versus what counts

the waters we rig
— excuse me
swim or drink
hold the map of knowledge
but we can only see them
in the stars
burning beyond years
as we chase them in the
extinction of humanity

Common Thread

We are a common thread in our
world's tongue
sung in different tonality,
humming various melodies to
our children —
newly reincarnated spirits
remember their heritage

Perhaps it is why Arabic
is al-knowing versed in poetry
or
why Chinese and Japanese
intently carve connection in
kanji
how we educate in English
sing in Spanish

Why we look to the sands of
time through Sanskrit
see the silk road through
Swahili

From our Ancestral seeds
we gather around a common
grain
yet bones replaced bread

I thought you were my reward for everything I'd been through. But you were just more to go through.
—Mari Andrew

Fragments

They sat at a booth in my
section

67 years of partnership

The ease of their laughter
carried over

They shared wisdom I already
knew

Communicate, not complicate

Don't settle in unresolved soil

But find partnership

Firm believers in longevity
because of each other

Stubbornly

I'm quietly dying from a broken
heart

You're alive but very well gone

No one else fits my front frame

Nor my windows welcome

Even when I slammed the door
— twice

Each time you return

A gentle reminder of the
universe

And still, I question how it
works

Did I ever thank you for saving
my life?

Your presence was a present of
spiritual growth

In the times we held each other
in darkness

Only to see our light

Not just another man or woman

A reminder of the entire
universe

And still, I question how it
works

Did I ever thank you for
breathing in new life?

I'm still mad

Today, seeing where my
replacement stands

Or simply stood up for me

As I'm worth fighting for

If I gave more a damn

After multiple times I flew to
you

And you sought someplace else

Did I lose you because I was
unsure of myself?

This question spirals out of my
pages

Perhaps out of context

No desire to be your cover girl

Not the first or only

Just important

As important as you are to me

How we didn't know our
existence

Before we existed

Unlocking the freedom of
falling

In love

With everything the light
touches

The outlines of our shadows

Constructing a sanctuary

Disassembled in seconds

Did I ever thank you for
transforming this anger into
art?

The weight of waiting for you
presses through window pains

Perhaps I hold anger in the
truth

In my inability to hold an entire
universe

As easily as in your arms

How many lifetimes

Will we continue to collect
pieces

Before we become a whole?

I could be anything in the world,
but I wanted to be his — Rupi Kaur

Distant Future Memories

The presence of falling in love
with him
still lingers on my sheets
in every other favorite dish
the soft good morning sex of no
sound

How he lay buoyant on my
skin —
naked in words
expressed in a single touch
his smile
his laugh
sink into the center of the couch

I loved the way his hums cut
through silence
as we drove to our next
adventure

the comforting trust as he takes
the wheel
as the dashboard rests my heels
I'd dampen my fire to swim in
his calm water
he'd dance around my hearth—
complement each other

The once sad sofa sleep sessions
from another season
now replaced

The presence of falling in love
with myself
lifts from ruffled sheets
into my cup of tea
beautiful bed hair
bareback with no bra
"you a beaver cuz damn!"
taped to my bathroom mirror
window open

the wind carries my [jazz/deep
house/pirate folk/genre of the
day]
as I carry my love from you to
me

In the end,
the void I tried to fill for you
was a mirror of my own
reclaimed parts of me
abandoned
hold myself with tenderness
love the pieces left behind in
your quest

In the quiet that follows your
departure
I hear the whispers of a woman
the voice of a self I've long
ignored
calling me home

to the heart that holds me — my
own.

Home II

The future feels foreign now
that the presence of you...

               ...is the past.

He said, "You always felt like
home"

      the one who dismantled
      my foundation to flee

"This feels like home", the
other says

      who brought lights in
      just in time to leave

Both finding my love not
enough yet "an
overabundance"

My fear is falling for the one in
the middle for his words may
finally be the truth

My home was built for me

        not in comparison to
        another human being

The spare key

        wasn't an invitation to
        change me

If I am not

        the woman you seek
        then leave me be

My home was built for me

Chef's Kiss

You cooked for me
Said it didn't need to mean
anything
I didn't want another soup
But watching you cook
Is like seeing stars through a
telescope

You'd be the best match
If I wanted an extended family
You're the perfect date night
But in the morning
A reckless breakfast of
Splattered batter and grease
And I like my kitchen clean

I'm sorry.

Causing confusion

Leaning into you
So close to the perfect kiss
You're a good friend but
I'm not ready for anyone to
enter

You deserve someone who
savors a full course
Not a few bites
Someone who compliments the
chef
Not of the food
But because they love you

Reconnection can feel like
serendipity
When sometimes
It's the time in our lives
Where we're simply making
peace

Proud of you.
Pouring your pain into a pot
And I, my poetry
We are not meant to be
Even with no allergies
Believing I'm the right recipe
I'm not ready to step into
The magic you create in the
kitchen
What I'll miss –
A chef's kiss

Each Other's Diary

we've become each other's
diary
folding ourselves into margins
soft truths tucked between
pauses
every silence a line we've yet to
read aloud

your smile spills ink across my
memory
a chapter I revisit on restless
nights
we swap spoken word
digest them like unfinished
drafts

warm them on a January eve
you show me
poetry doesn't need a perfect
ending

we write this story quietly —
four a.m. tea
rooftop views of the city
inkless, timeless
a record of what matters
when nothing else is said

Labor Pains: A Letter to My Future Son/Daughter

Inhale. Exhale.
(Breathe) I know
Inhale. Exhale.
(Breathe) I *know*
Change can be painful
It will be *so* worth it my dear.

A contraction — a pause before
birth
what exists in that stillness?
trust, breath, surrender
pain becomes teacher

At first, you'll only know my
good side
eventually, the deeper parts of
me won't be so easy to hide
Please remember

I continuously rediscover my
reflection as I now view it from
you
the atom of our matter isn't as
important as why we matter
You are destined to be a better
version of me

It is written that you are a gift
from God
recycled to reveal the errors of
our ways
rebirthed as love
refreshed eyes of life
forgive me for being selfish as
you came from my flesh
divine miracles
independently your own

There will always be worry,
worry in the way

that I am never enough for you
unable to recognize the
melodies of my child's cries –
hungry harmonies, staccatos of
sickness and lack of sleep
or "woman, leave me in peace!"

Cradling this fragile joy in
trembling hands
adjusting to a new universe in
my personal space
learning my native language
without prior knowledge
how incredibly patient you are
to love someone who never felt
it before

Will you like your given name
or understand that to give you
everything
is at a cost, a sacrifice

we'll plan
yet the best
is to accept change

We will hurt each other
though I'll love you
even if you choose to murder
you will become the lesson in
let go

All you'll discover
Remember
You're a cosmic marvel

Dear Me

(Dedicated to and performed by the
'25 Berkeley Center of the Arts
Creative Writing Seniors)

Your perception will change

The people you love will
change

You will disagree — even argue

Just remember through the pain

Everyone is finding themselves

Don't take it too personally

Even if it's who you call family

You'll fall in love

You'll hold several broken
hearts

You'll carry that weight

My hope is that you'll continue
to lead the way

Back to love within you

It's not like the movies

But may they inspire you to
move

To try again

Travel beyond a tourist

Be open to someone else

Stand firm within yourself

You'll need to let go

Of what you know

To simply grow

Understand peace does not
equal happiness

I repeat

Peace does not equal happiness

It's okay to take a break

Find out what you're good at

What you fail at

You don't have to know
everything

And not everything is in the
palm of your hand

Embrace the messy parts of you

Remember that mistakes don't
define you

And, no, it's not the end of the
world

Learn to be alone without being
lonely

Learn financial literacy so you
can be free

At times go crazy but trust your
instincts

Life will be overwhelming so
get some sleep

Nutrition doesn't come in a
powder, box, or take-away

Attempt a cooking connection

You don't need a membership
to workout

But your body needs to move

So find your rhythm

May these challenges become
the catalysis

Out of a comfortable cocoon

For you are the biggest light
when your world gets dark

Losing a soulmate is a different type of heartache

Pawprints

To bite, or not to bite, that is the
question

Intentionally
just out of reach attention
seekers
guardians of the door
gifts left on the floor
purrs that produce protection
or pride in their new "art"
collection

Pawprints are the love letters
written in the language of
stolen items and toppled plants
their mischief spilling over the
pages — ink that refuses to stay
in line

Their automatic entitlement to
talk back
purrrcussion purrrfectionists
needing just the right
purrrsition to plop

Savor the selection of your lap
the safety of their slumber
tufts of confetti fur
leftover love in their absence
how a small magician takes up
all this space
purposely tripping you
as you fall in love

Pawprints are the love letters
written in the language of
kneading your knots
unthreading your couch
Their mischief becomes a
memory

softened by the sounds of
meow

They greet death well before we
realize its near
hiding their pain to protect us
from doing the same
letting them go is
so damn hard
like finding all their hidden
spaces
or catching them in mid sprint

Either way leave the door ajar
shall this spirit guardian choose
to return to you

Hi Friend,

Would sending you a letter cause unease? Would a text or phone call have you pressing ignore me? I'm not even sure if you need me. Patiently being present, sitting with you in silence that was once a symphony. I'll repeat what you once said to me on a cold, rainy eve:

Please, please, *don't disappear*.

That's all you said, I'll add, don't disappear like clouds we cannot see that come back with wet weight. You once asked why I wasn't selfish; believe me underneath all that giving, I constantly crave unspoken assurance. If not wanting to lose you falls into that category, then I am tremendously selfish. It would be like losing the innocence of befriending someone on the first day of school. As a woman who once stood on the beach holding a trigger, betrayed by those she thought truly loved her, I understand.

I'll be here whether you need to break down into ash, I'll bring the match. Or rebuild, I'll bring bricks. Some soul mates are problem solvers to see ourselves. Or to bear into the soils of our souls, remind us we are home.

Or simply say, I understand.

As a woman who once stood on the beach holding a trigger, betrayed by those she thought truly loved her, I understand. Even with all the copious opportunities, I too, struggle. Feel free to borrow a piece of this heart while yours is breaking. Don't hide, your affectionate affirmation glows. Behind the darkness you are what the world gains in growth.

One thing I won't say is, "how are you?'

How heavy those words weigh when you want to slip in the door, be unrecognized yet seen. Be heard yet not having to speak. I love you seems saturated or miscalculated. I don't need to say it because I'm right here to let you know. To stand right here is living proof of these depressing thoughts, my friend, you can slay them.

Friend Ships

To the friends that refine us
without redefining us

Through time do we know how
important we are

Tethered to stand the test of
misunderstandings

Family gatherings

And romantic pursuits

Our differences at a distance

We call our significant partners
our best friends

Yet we turn to our deepest to be
honest

Yes, some will sail

Cause a few masts to tear

For the few that can stand the
journey

No sea will restrain a friend
ship

I can go outside and feel something. That's humidity. Art is supposed to split us open and transform us. —Benny Starr

Trip Over Our Truths

(Excerpt for "Unseen Struggles" from
the album *Verse Vibes* by Zachery
Williams)

How we lie down for lies
open up for the obvious
makeover for media but trip
over our truths
break the ice from our devices
disconnecting us by connecting
us to walls
mistake confidence cringing in
crumbled candor
guilty over being alive while
loved ones turn to suicide

Don't be afraid to turn over
new leaves

put on the kettle to pour for the
table
rebuild burned bridges
meet in the middle
pass by in peace
relearn to walk
lean into listening
scrape your knees
As you rediscover
b r e a t h i n g.

Our Ten Minutes of Fear is A News Article's "Minor Altercation"

May 27, 2024

A few nights ago, I watched blood come out of a man's mouth, seconds after being shot. For a moment, the entire restaurant was silent. Then everyone ran, including myself. The fear of being shot in the back rose because seeing clearly through chaos isn't an option.

We tried to hide behind cars but people were driving away. The shooter followed then drove dangerously between scores of us. Their car came our way, accelerating in a zigzag. Fragments of fear settled in as determining the direction of our jump meant survival.

How one person's inability to control their anger led to the emotional instability of a lifetime of trauma for others.

Our youngest member was barely able to breathe, choking on her hyperventilation. Holding her, I said to breathe with me, then call her parents. I held so many of them.

She giggled over yogurt when we collectively decided to band together the day after. Yet she'll forever battle the nightmares and the choice to return as the pressure points linger.

And *She*, who bravely held a man struggling to stand, walked away with a blood-stained shirt. A mark of heroes but a mark of injustice to a young woman's innocence.

Heal from Hate II

even when she hated what i
created

i adored her

so much love, hidden in pain

unable to find outside of her
hate

i'd call her

a sisterly cadence in the comfort
of her voice

for me it was at airports
between layovers

somehow she knew i was alone

sneaking in our conversations
among her confinerary

i miss her

may we find peace in the
broken pieces

that reflect our relationship i've
attempted to patch

much like the lack of postcards
in an airport

is our existence enough

to remove these wounds that
once bound us in anger

as we seek to recover?

Sandwich

Before the franchised Subways, there was Sub Station and my grandmother would take me there on a few occasions.

I had moved from Colorado to Alabama, and nothing made sense. In the mountains, we had a garden, and my mom cooked and baked, we rarely went out.

Now that family life was changing rapidly, fast food was our new normal. What better way to spend time with family than to eat. My grandmother's favorite past time.

We stood in line, and I barely saw over the glass covered containers of veggies and meats. I didn't know what to order, much less how to order. I went with what I knew, which was probably just meat and cheese.

Skipping over the toppings, grandmother groaned, "Abigirl, that's what makes a *sandwich* a *sandwich*." I'm not sure what I ate or attempted to eat as I'm sure my grandmother ordered for me.

Although she passed on, the wisdom in her words as an adult stick clearly. It's the little bit of pepper in the perk of my loved ones' laughter, the spilling of tea with close friends, and the little moments in between the mundane that fill in our sandwiches. I believe that's why they become our comfort food or crave them with a side of soup. I love them but hold the onions.

What would poetry be

without you or me?

would I be a late discoverer or
none at all?

would I find a different muse?

would I stay lost at sea or find a
different home?

would I stunt my growth?

would I ignore all the
uncomfortable signs to
eventually find comfort?

I wouldn't know

for

I've become my own tree.

Playwright

ACT I

have you ever rolled down a
hill

full speed on a bike

or kissed someone in the rain

not a peck

an in-the-moment intent

or jumped out of a plane

you don't have to…

…to fall in love

ACT III

how deep my mind goes

to envy those with injuries

that wipe their memories

unveil

the sight of your realization

that you are forgotten

just a pang of pain

of how you saw me

Scene

I held the door open for you

You chose one closed

It's beautiful what you made

Deep down I know she once
was me

Always welcoming you home

And you broke it

So it's no wonder it's not even a
thought

Of making her dinner,
showering her in flowers, being
distant yet together

As I stand here saying what the
hell happened

Once a week I see her sitting in
traffic

Always with her hair down

Perfectly layered with a tint of a
wave

Fiddling with her cap or phone

We seem to be at a similar focal
point

Just moments between points A
and B

Funny, we used to share a C

Now it just haunts me

A reminder of the woman I'll
never be

We both deserve grace

We both deserve peace

Even if I continue to wonder

What did you learn from me?

END SCRIPT

Essence

"You seem so happy!"

It's really the peace I've made
with everything/the blueprint
of my new rhythm of how to
breathe

finally gaining my
independence

see, no one tells you that to
become at ease is to break
down piece by piece

no one ever tells you in the
midst of deep dark depression
especially when you're single

you have to *hold* you

you have to *love* you

there's no backup/no matter
how many gaps you try to fill

and if it's just happiness you
can have it/I guarantee you
cannot sit in your silence

I can

it's the bounce back not always
the balance

So, no

I'm not chasing something that
only comes in waves/in the
swells and surf, it's about the
relationship that you gain

A standing testament to suicide
while so many others failed

the sliver of selfishness not
wanting to share/to pout like a
toddler and say it isn't fair

or that my worth isn't devalued
when I feel like a broken record
ignoring the voice saying go do
you/over-singing this chorus of
I'm not enough

even as my former lover still
takes the time to care as I
compare myself to who he has
chosen

or when I can't correctly
articulate the many plates I
hold on each arm as I navigate
serving you food and food for
thought

poetry stems from my physical
movement otherwise, I st st
stutter if I st stand still

doctors said she needs Ritalin
mom knew better, children just
need an outlet to breathe in

don't ask how I remember
minute details or conduct
business

when brain fog screams "we
need a decision!"

overstimulated situations slip
by in seconds

as I return months later to
collect them

did you seam my fabrics as you
tell me how I seem to feel?

do I owe you joy because we
share pain?

these mountains I move help
motivate not just me but
hopefully you

allow me my rest and time to
myself

where you see happiness I see
peace

navigate your burdens like the
ocean, leave only with saltwater
and sand — not emotion

the encapsulation of all this
growth quickly became a
flashback film to show

the original love I always held
one I now can purposely tell of
the essence of my existence

Doughnuts

I don't like
the taste of doughnuts

I broke one with you anyway
to try and taste the sweetness of
your lips; undo this morning's
burnt toast and the jam
imported jealousy

Forgive me for being a bit
overprotective I'm still new to
your perspective, protecting an
asset that

molds me
reminds me
to curse less
but please

Be patient with my soul

As a poet once said,
drop the e and just go
be patient as I lay
down my foundation

One you may seek while out
gallivanting
I see it as you request a presence
at each endeavor
the scan of your eyes
across multiple dance partners

It's why I allow a pass
every time you ask,
'Do you like coffee?'
when you know damn well,
I am Divine Tea

Trust me

I'm willing to let you slip
under this skin
there's more to navigating
my body's geography
beyond milk and honey
the garden of growing pains
forbidden fruit forced from its
foundation
bruised berries that might still
be succulent
if you know exactly how to suck
them

So lay me down like jazz —
slow, deliberate,
letting every note linger
until it becomes more than
sound

trace the topography of this
fragile body

Take this skin
this sweetness
never sought but now crave
like the doughnut we broke —
imperfect,
sticky with glaze,
a mess worth the indulgence

Dare to Ask Me What I Speak

because I don't throw

on a dress or heels or

let down my hair

you'd never know that I speak

mambo, salsa, a bit of

swing, splash of tango, bachata,

cha-cha slide into a country line

foxtrot or freestyle

you'd never know

because

no one

dares to

ask if I

dance

Been Writing These Poems

to rest and refocus
continuously ask what is my
purpose?
help me forget all the turbulence
when this engine starts to jet
when rock bottom looks like
above water
on rafts of regrets floating in
failure
of that which I face
but not a definition of what I
tailor
i pull these lines out of time
the closest to touching planets in
the sky
understanding another universe
the value of love and patience
soul searching through verse

poetry of that I call my partner
is really myself, rediscovered
this Divine Being steeped in
beau-tea been writing these
poems helping shape humanity
the lifeline of poetry

Though this be the last pain that she makes me suffer and these the last verses that I write for her. — Pablo Neruda

These Lines

These lines I wrote out of time
for you shall never be returned

A currency I can no longer
afford to spend

eventually I'll need space for
someone else

The voided mass flooded with
memories

Forgetting

The most important relation is
one with myself

Flashback to our first meeting

You asked me if different countries are greener

I told you then the more you do you, the right people will come along

While searching outside yourself, you didn't mean any harm

You found your inner self among the casing of your outer shell

Left under the rubble of burned bridges as you hang family frames of your soul space

You're the best mountain I've ever climbed / trusting in time as you moved on, and I, across states

Remembering the lines of your open soul removing the curtains to my window

May the next season of life be so grand as to give reason why we no longer stand

How to let someone go — intertwined, a rock through difficult times

Setting boundaries where our misunderstandings landed on fault lines we daringly danced across

Surely, not all regrets

Remember you once claimed
my house, your home,
becoming family unable to turn
to our own

Searching

Naïvely

Believing

I can be meaning

Of I love you

How important to a man once so
selfish never felt shame
apologizing – stop me from

wasting my time as he took up so much of mine

To the man that became my best friend: was our purpose our pain or celebrate all that we gained?

For these lines, these lines shall be the last I remove from time

Of the life we've given to each other

Of the light we've projected

Of all that we made

Perhaps our time now

Is to part ways

My soul is a hidden orchestra; I know not what instruments, what strings and harps, drums and tamboura I sound and clash inside myself. I only know myself as a symphony. —Fernando Pessoa

Theme Song

she's an angel
no need for wings
so small in the grand scheme of
things
holds your entire soul

her smile is the makeup that
paints her face etched by
wrinkled squints burst into
laughter

she's tough; fights her own fire
leaving rough edges but look
close enough
she's the softest to touch

easily   distracted   and
overexcited
just give her some space

craves other cities
rushes to catch them
just to come back and relive
them
her favorite, though, is the one
she created

soaks up the smell of fresh cut
grass after a good rain
if you listen, you can hear her
sing

her hugs are the safe harbor of
your pain
the prism of your love—an
unspoken exchange

overwhelmingly compassionate
deeply dipped thoughts into
depression

to not care at all is easy for
others
but for her damn near
impossible

All the things I (re)discovered
dating myself

I'm unclear what being Native American means.
I have no tribe ties or knowledge passed down. For
my sister it was adorning barren walls with
windchimes and sleeping under wolf print covers.
For my father, it was something he never questioned
but had no memory (at least in this lifetime)
Perhaps it's the same as knowing where to be
or deja vu? For me it's cultural dissonance more
than discovery. Perhaps it's why I never braid
my hair or leave it down for that matter. The
same feeling when I'm too embarrassed (?)
to speak Spanish. As it, too, is apart of me
I never fully embraced.

Common Thread II

If you gave me a map

I wouldn't know how to read it

or tell you the direction we're
headed

I count stars but can't name
them

My father's parents

or at least their parents

once had common thread

to what we call Colorado

I never believed in generational
trauma

until I understood the
dislocation

of their route from Native
American

to orphanage

to child abuse

I saw the psychological
aftermath

indented on the bathroom door

of their house

I hear the struggle of my aunts'
voices

as they continue to find
themselves

trickled down to my sister and
me

forgotten how to weave

Ripped from mother nature's
handbook

all we have left in this modern
world

is someone else's language

even still misinterpreted

I write other biographies

in search of my own

be it wolves or dreamcatchers

they adorn my sister's home

it's not too late for us to dream

It's not too late to weave

foreign knowledge

in our quilt's thread

as we to return to Diné Tah

As another poet once read

I now believe

generational trauma

can end with me

Kujikomboa

My tea and I speak

Steam curling like the whispers
of a past

One that no longer weighs me
down

An unsung song of someone
solo

Once the outside of an inside
joke

Now water for growth

Formerly drowning in my
ancestors' rivers

Taught me to swim in drought

Sustain the seeds of my success

Plants that push through

Painting my present

Coloring my future

With each sip, Tea transports me

To the passport of places I get to tell

Of people who hold no currency

Rich in humanity for worth is not measured

The world demands a hearty
stew

Pressuring us, simmering for it
to consume

But Tea speaks of the spice, of
fragrance, the bitterness,

Chilled or steamed for us to
choose

To liberate ourselves from the
pressure we are cooked under

Many years in silence

Always borrowing from my
future

Held down by my captors

Whom I now forgive

I cup the warmth

To soothe the former shouts of
my voice

Now speaks volumes in silence

Of the woman who ran away

To grow

To gather

Claim herself whole

Tamashii no Tomo

where

have you been all my life?

am I

supposed to ask you the same?

is that

what soulmates really say?

your silence stings like an
unanswered question

or maybe sings

an entire day

where our eyes say hello

our mouths feed from each
other's plate

the cursive lettering of our
fingerprints

two separate entities

fused chemistry

elemental individuality

should it

always be dubbed romantically

this terminology

we call serendipity

we can be the lighthouse of
those between ships

keepers against falling into the
shadows

of themselves

while staying strong

as loving someone else

shows us the value of the self

we can be the lighthouse of
those between ships

despite the wreckage we bring

holding space

for the versions of us

yet to arrive

in between

we are not perfect or permanent

certainly

too damn special to be seasonal

the safety in that stillness

the warmth even at a distance

an encourager of who I can be

if can just see

the lighthouse within me

"I don't yet know how to help you connect, but maybe, if we meet, something will spill over in conversation" — *Tethered Wrds*

Common Thread III

I like to believe

I don't fix the narratives

I'm asked to edit

I like to believe

my arrangement

of their words

is enough

to keep their views

to share in success and pain

that I see their value

Although

I cannot make them

accept their reflection

Have we confused empathy
with sympathy

is it worth sharing all we
experience

do we give ourselves the silence

to digest something new

evolve from what we know

can we listen intently

not take such burdens home

where small acts of kindness
are easy

compared to the progression of

removing negative imprints

we've been given

There's simply no space

to decompress

between cultures and countries

prescribed perspectives

vs

the dosage

To go on living in your comfort zone

when it challenges everything known

many continue to make peace through pain

while we fight over misspelled names

How do we break the cycle and bridge the circle?

not every question possesses an answer

so easy to throw money at a problem — that's all we have

it's our way of not wanting to
step into a mess

when we build structures

and then take the tools to
maintain

false hope is all that remains

we forget how easy it is

to return to the way we are

When you know no borders, you have the luxury of common sense
— *Bill Weir*

6/23/2025

Iran. Palestine. Armenia. When — no I dare not
ask for as long as humans exist, war will remain.
I don't blame Allah for what we fail to remember.
The divinity in all of us, that our differences make
us better. That our worth isn't weighed in oil, gold
or water but in each other.

They have shown me forgiveness
A comfort within pain
~~Maybe even love~~
Now we must do the same.

Barakah II

Iran. Palestine. Armenia.
Ukraine. Syria. Sudan. Congo.

Shall I go on?

When — no I dare not ask for as
long as humans exist, war will
remain.

I don't blame Allah for what we
fail to remember.

The divinity in all of us

That our differences make us
better

That our worth is not weighed
in

Oil, gold, or water

Only in each other

They have shown us
forgiveness

A comfort within conflict

Now we must do the same

In the Land of More Pens than Palmettos

(Dedicated to the 2025 Soda City
Poetry Festival and the current
vacancy of state laurate)

A myriad of poets collect in the
state capital

While we bring no
megaphones, banners

We do bring the fighting spirit

We, too, have been selected to
represent our community

Persistent conversations, no
forced interactions

We listen to our elders,
understand our youth

Aim to protect our future

While there is no seat at the
table of congress for us

We make diplomacy believable
again

When asked what we did for
history

We proudly state we are Poets
—no explanation needed

Summer Reading

screens replaced screened
porches

a moment in silence to listen to
the birds sing

mosquitos surrounding gossip
buzzing

attempting to remove scent
strip us of self

circadian rhythms incarcerated
for the crime of existing

private prayer on public
display getting in the way of
purpose

when we were younger

not telling the truth

got us in trouble

even adults need supervision

as lies are the new foundation

the only ban i wanna see

is the rubber stuck in one's hair

learning to braid, make
ponytail

giggling over stories — ghosts
and fairytales

water balloons and pillow
fights

allowing generations before us

to rest as they fought for our
rights

fireflies engulfed in wildfires

so we can play god with just a
switch

be home for dinner

but the streetlights are always
on

we've confused the moon with
the sun

in this land

we hold the gold

not the kind to be sold

the invisible ticket of

contributions transferable into
citizenship

wrapped in freedom of speech

continue telling your story

as they sell your home

Highwater creative power
come together

before our words are banned

Marvels

I carry a bag of marbles
interlace my fingers in the mesh
They sat in a cigar box next to
important documents
and foreign currency

I'm not here to trade them
instead, I play each one like
film strips –
from the smallest scene
you silently stand my
toothbrush upright
that lay on the side of the sink

To the midsized swirls of
holding your hand
as you cried in confidence at a
Red Robbins

A piggyback in Publix
my favorite and
how you never
snore in your sleep
only smile

Then there's the biggest
a tiny universe
the creator of ripples
seeing us again for the first time

I'm silly to hold onto them
perhaps my memories became
marbles because
you drove me crazy
I bury them in the ground
return the earth's minerals
as I say goodbye

Favorite Color

"That's the silliest thing I've ever heard," as she follows in laughter.

He confides to his niece that he sometimes lies to himself.

She takes his hand and shows him there's no monsters under the bed.

"Do you truly believe you're unworthy because one person you loved left you?"

I pause.

I expect a lecture, but he hands
me a mirror and waits.

I'm here to tell you

Truth is my favorite color

so be who you are

where there may not be trust

there is still love in each other.

This piece is rooted from sexual assault trauma, but my hope is that it leaves an inspirational impression more so than a painful memory. If you or someone you know is suffering, please consider T.R.I. County Speaks, RAINN.org, and/or your local hospital.

Heal from Hate III

twenty-eight times

my body

became another's property

withered by unwanted hands

left naked in the shower

subdued into their laughter

how does a girl now grow

given too early the knowledge
of womanhood

blood and bone beyond a
textbook

become so uncomfortable

cutting her skin

anything

to thicken

this new definition

of pain

young lady

naïvely

carries it over

what she sees in the mirror

as she takes another
backhanded hit

starts to fall into the pattern

if i do what they say

maybe they'll go away

so how do you heal from such
hate?

stop pretending to love what
kills you

remove yourself from the
environment

even if you couch surf your
way

stop feeding the fungus

so your future can find focus

cut those relationship ties

cry yourself to sleep

so the next morning

you can rise

break things

be angry

but don't beat yourself up

as you start to open up

and undo this hate they create

learn to live alone

lean into those who listen

sit in your silent sanctuary

dig deep into your soil

before you allow another soul
in

hug yourself

so love can rejuvenate

all the scars the body creates

the body that keeps the score

of this woman is no longer
worn

she can breathe in new energy

she can talk in therapy

she can shed skin

so the next generation

can learn to heal from their hate

The Purpose

Generational trauma, how tired
you must be

to view success as a serpent to
slay

when it can be your cue to
finally sleep

taking up a reincarnated
residency

turning our bodies into hotels

wearing it down to a hospital

driving us to psychological
paranoia.

"There's something wrong with me"

was

just

you

screaming.

Generational anger, how tired
you must be

not to be seen as beauty

I am *so, so* sorry

Generational grief, how tired
you must be

searching for a moment to
breathe but it's safe now

You can release for I am the last
body you hold

and the first prisoner to be
transformed

Generational ancestor, I thank
you.

Through poetry and prayer, I
see you as a separate entity
from me

I understand why you came
how you traveled centuries

Perhaps you're the source

of myths that never find love:

Pandora's Box,

       curiosity and blame

Aphrodite,

       worshipped never fully
       loved

Isis and Osiris,

       longing for wholeness

the headless horseman,

       a restless run

They became the stories we tell
ourselves:

of the beauty we lack

the love we don't deserve

everything

that

isn't

true

Generational greeter, I grant
you your freedom from your
internal prison

may you rest in peace instead
of protest

although I exile your existence
from your mountain I am a
purpose

Home III

a part of me

believes

you'll walk up

my sidewalk

or

leave a sign

in my absence

i miss you

the

unquestionable accent

of your soul

i must accept

you may never return

and it will be okay

whoever

comes after you

will not fill any shoes

i'll see them

for them

and you

for you

my home awaits

the next endeavor

as it does

my daily return

temporary.

I want to find peace like the water who hold rip currents, underneath chaos is truly still. Water — no matter the form is chronically bombarded by, probed + prodded, by ~~mistaken~~ diving birds, jumping fish, cutting boats, storing the stories we wish to hide like dead bodies or ~~bullshit~~ make believe wishing well. Yet when water preserve builds it rebuilds the earth. It reminds us to show some respect, not just for it but our bodies too.

7:00 pm.
5 - ~~29~~ - 2025

A moment of silence for all the reminders of how easy it is to quit on yourself. How easy it is to not show up or even get out of bed or leave the house. How quickly ~~we're~~ ~~can~~ ~~be~~ we become hard on ~~you~~ ourselves over one remark, one mistake we are walking reminders of our past, our pain, our purpose. Sometimes we forget that we are the present.

Shape of Water

I wish I knew love without him
　　yet I'd never learn
　　to love all the parts of me

Longing to hold the shape
　　of what you call art
　　I call memories

To love like water
　　deep and nourishing
　　let it slip out of one's
fingers

The same hands
　　that cup liquid
　　that hold another human

At times we bury

these elements
as we search
what already holds us

Peaceful river
        holds rip currents
        chronically bombarded,
poked and prodded
        underneath chaos truly
still

Storing the stories
        we wish to hide like
dead bodies
        or make believe wishing
wells

Take a moment of silence
        for all the exit signs
        that could have erased
your existence

Dust

Lost in translation

Avalanched

Mountain of memories or is it
mistakes?

When pens could go past the
date

Where no sound could speak

The ghosts in galleries

Echo chambers

Broken records

Static between us

Replaces the silence

Sought comfort in

Warped, never fixed

Forgot the language

Recall

Breaking bread

Not boundaries

Appetizers of appreciation

Where distance

Was dessert

When we fell for fondness

When trust was believable

When simple sayings didn't
turn selfish

When dust danced instead of
burned

Honesty II

If the truth sets us free
Why do I feel so guilty
Grieving the possibility
Now a blank canvas of could
haves
The curtains of boundaries
Become blurry when the small
acts of kindness
Overshadows the truth of
settling for less
Less than someone's full
presence

In a world where agreeability is
favored over authenticity
Many of you believe in a brand
before yourselves

The confusion of my light
switch burns bridges
Open arms
Aren't enough for the patience I
lack
Teatime throws away my
assumptions
Spills the moment a lack of
trust is present

Don't ask me to repeat myself
My aggression is self-alignment
The challenge of being human
When honesty is mistaken for
harm

If Peace Could Speak

I acknowledge your presence
what is sacred to you is valid
even if it's not mine

This land holds your ancestors'
memories as it does theirs
restore the human story
we are remnants of earth dust
and water but move like wind
yet you choose who lives

before boarders and religions
we were just people so how does
your faith call you to love
strangers?

does it exist in your scripture or
repaint pain? perhaps civic
policy over a divine belief can
bring an end to injustice

Tangency

linear equation relationships

never cross

parallel partnerships

equal ceased

connection or crossing
intersection

how many in curved bells

stayed disguised as constant
variables?

star alignments are simple

choices to move, to stay

to catch a train

the bravery to greet a person

or opportunity

or to let go

of all you know

in continued growth

there's more strands of sand

than stars in the galaxy

of all the hauntingly beautiful

weirdly explained sea and sky

i'm simply grateful

you found my poetry

Knowing One Another

A sigh of relief

I held you to high standards

Wanting you to be permanent

You hold the pressure of potential in all you do

So damn precious but just a pivot

deeply loving you at a distance

I forgive you, albeit may never tell you

Can the future stand next to my fire without flinching?

Become the perimeter so it can shine brighter?

One I may overlook for simplicity

The gift is in the resonance, not the performance

Emotional range with steadiness

I ask myself, are you ready for this?

I think that I shall never see a poem lovely as a tree — Joyce Kilmer

A Soul's Tree

two writers carve three lines in
four months
a friendship ring forms deep
roots in a haiku —

Travel
Down the roots
Taller

in the inhaled high of our
weirdness,
Poets pick soul food from their
soils
to potluck in the collective
shade

through the eyes of his
daughter,
I see heaven
not in scripture

but in the way she reaches for
him
in the way laughter,
generations later, carries over

my soul's tree
is marked by the handprints left
in bark
carved by the seeds of my
ancestors
framed in the mosaic of my
loved ones
spoken in no language but sung
from any tongue

breathes in her serenity
as we stretch
under her oak tree

shedding skin
for a photographer's lens
revealing beauty within

my bare branches

sap together memories
now soaked tea leaves
once floating down
spinning rapidly
softly landing on her couch

cat resting at my roots
purring
in patience
I rarely give myself

my soul hums
her harp in the hallway
of this wood
taking root
woven into this family's nest

my sisters in song
hold another version of me
I had forgotten about

perhaps a messenger
a guide
look to the tree top

now yourself — home

Italian and Palestinian Olive,
Spanish Moss, English Oak,
German Beech
Ombú y Guanacaste
gather 'round
sharing fruitful knowledge

no religion needed to explain
the divinity I see in all of them

we're elongated seasons
all too sacred
trees of memories
ancient witnesses
an unspoken part of the self

at times, cannot see the light
among the forest
I worry
who shall I be on the other side
of it
carrying the weight of the fallen

a network of
nutrient-aid knowledge

depression is apart of me
I surrender only that
it does not be my definition

I can move mountains
tell the truth in times of trouble
be not the answer but the
example

parts of my bark become
paper — the pages of chapters
some I can't close as they sit
in my psyche
wrote the ending for me

the axe to the heart
when love
rooted
turns
leaves

listen to the bend in the wind
you'll find the connection
between
forest and ocean

among them I am told world
peace starts with a tidy home

although I am but human
my soul, my soul
is a giving tree

What does your soul's tree look
like?

It's everything you've ever
dreamed of
but never pictured before

There are so many of you, *far* too many of you to thank for shaping this person and publication. Whether you've asked me to perform, joined me for tea, booked a service, connected throughout the community, helped me get by, or simply held this book, my sincere gratitude.

www.ingramcontent.com/pod-product-compliance
Lightning Source LLC
Chambersburg PA
CBHW051307120626
46547CB00015B/2120